French-Horn Player

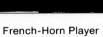

Recorder

Bass Drummer

Conductor

Concert Singers

Harpsichord (French, 1747)

Operatic Soloist

Bell Player

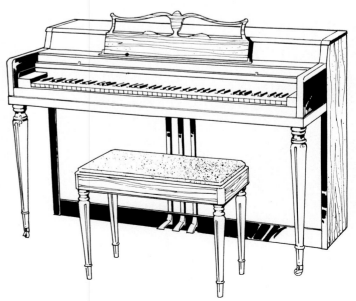

Piano (Spinet)

3

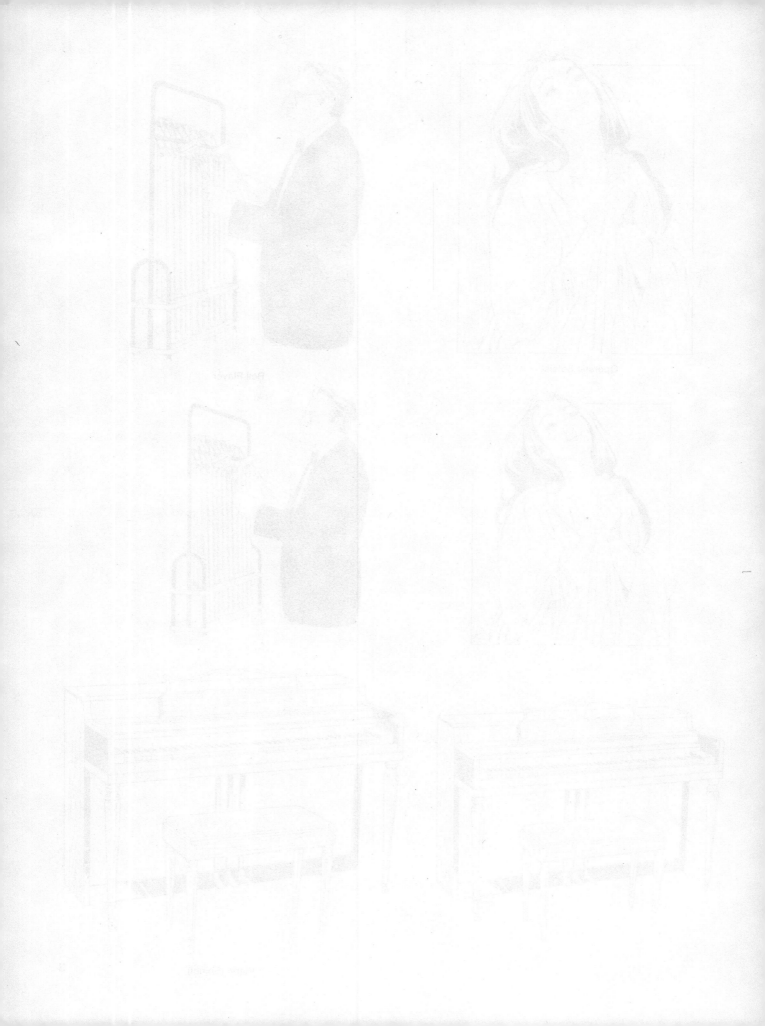

String Quartet

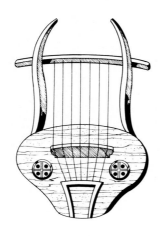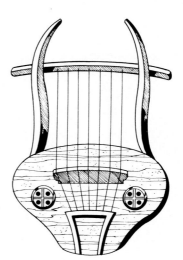

Lyre

Wind Quintet

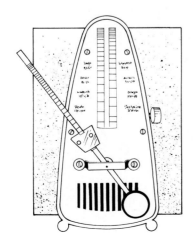

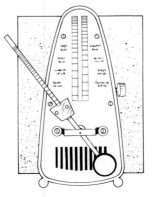

Metronome

Operatic Trio

Trumpet

　Piano Teacher

Violist

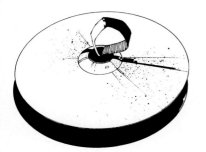

Cymbals

Pianist

7

Bass Trombonist

Tubist

Lutenist

Trumpeter

Bassoon

Classical Guitarist

Bassoonist

Trombone

Johann Sebastian Bach

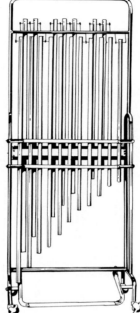

Richard Wagner

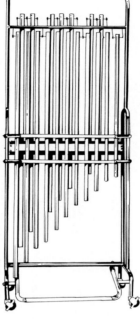

Orchestral Bells

Johannes Brahms

Guitar

Bass Trombone

Franz Schubert

Giuseppe Verdi

Pipe Organ

Wolfgang Amadeus Mozart

Chorus

Ludwig van Beethoven

Serpent

Bass Clarinetist

Contrabassoonist

Double Bass Player

Xylophonist

Flute

Clarinetist

Piccolo

Clarinet

Oboe

Cymbal Player

Bass Clarinet

Theorbo

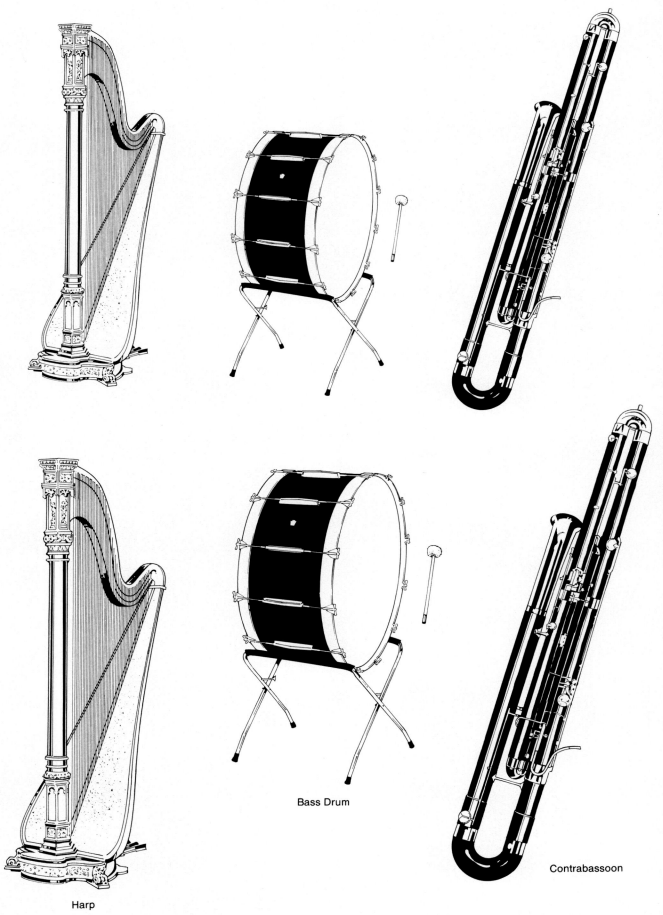

Harp

Bass Drum

Contrabassoon

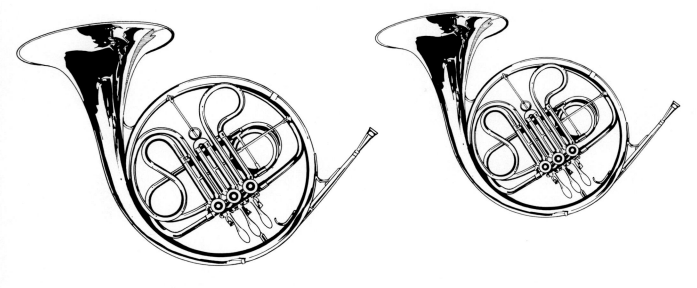

French Horn

Side Drum

Kettledrum

Piccolo Player

English Horn

Viola

Violin

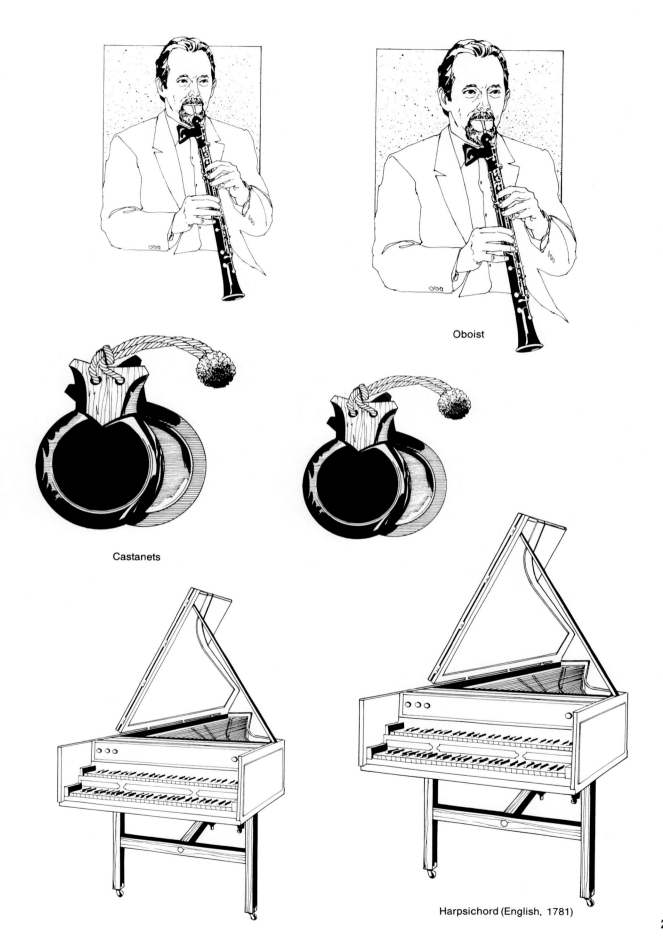

Oboist

Castanets

Harpsichord (English, 1781)

23

Double Bass

Cello

Side Drummer

Triangle Player

Clarinetist

Clavichord

Tuba

Concert Singer

Piccolo Player

Conductor

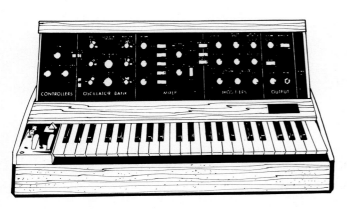

Portable Synthesizer

Flutist

Symphony Orchestra

English-Horn Player

Trombonist

Sheet Music (Instrumental Part)

Trumpeter

Violinist

Chorus

Conductor

Timpanist

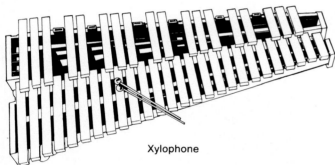
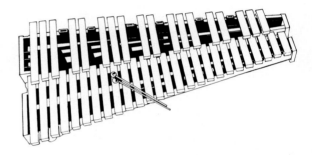

Xylophone

Harpist

Grand Piano

Triangle (with Striker)

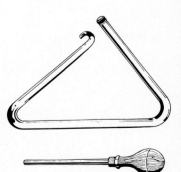

Lieder Singer